Original title:
Banana Sunsets

Copyright © 2025 Creative Arts Management OÜ
All rights reserved.

Author: Theodore Sinclair
ISBN HARDBACK: 978-1-80586-338-0
ISBN PAPERBACK: 978-1-80586-810-1

Basking in Warmth's Embrace

Golden glow upon my face,
Chasing shadows, a silly race.
Fruits in hand, laughter flows,
Even the night can't steal our shows.

Silly hats and giggles ring,
We dance like monkeys, wild and spring.
Sun drops low, a playful tease,
With every slip, we laugh with ease.

The Palette of Nightfall

Colors splash, a wacky sight,
Painted clouds in fading light.
Lemon-yellow, pinkish hue,
Strawberry dreams we once knew.

A purple burst, a splashy grin,
As daylight winks, our joys begin.
We swirl in hues, our voices loud,
Wacky friends, we stand so proud.

Twilight's Juicy Secrets

In the twilight, secrets bloom,
Laughter bounces, filling the room.
Melon whispers, so absurd,
Silly tales, we twist each word.

Orange skies, a fruity mess,
Giggles echo, we can't suppress.
Under these hues, we plot and scheme,
In sunset's glow, we chase our dream.

Last Light Over Lush Fields

Fields aglow with golden fun,
Chasing shadows one by one.
Animals dance and giggle around,
As the last light spills on the ground.

Crickets chirp their evening tune,
Underneath the smiling moon.
We hold hands and jump with glee,
This is where we long to be.

Solstice of Sweetness

On a pier of yellow dreams,
Laughter echoes, or so it seems.
Silly monkeys dance in line,
While juicy fruits sip on wine.

Cotton candy clouds above,
Belly laughs and quirky love.
Sunshine giggles, a playful tease,
Waving at the evening breeze.

Radiance Over Water

Ripples shimmer in a trance,
Fish start popping, join the dance.
Glimmers twinkle, cheeky sprites,
Splashing colors, silly sights.

Waves wink back with citrus glee,
A party set for you and me.
Boats are sailing with a grin,
While frolicking dolphins dive right in.

Daydreams in Citrus Tones

Sunkissed cheeks in shades so bright,
Chasing shadows, pure delight.
Lemon slices, a quirky crew,
Swirl around, just me and you.

Whispers carried on the breeze,
Tickling toes and buzzing bees.
Orange whispers, giggles sound,
As zestful dreams start to abound.

Nature's Golden Canvas

Brushstrokes of a playful land,
Where silly creatures roam so grand.
Pineapple hats on every head,
With laughter blooming, joy widespread.

Sunbeams painting, golden hue,
Twinkling winks from skies so blue.
Every corner tells a joke,
As nature grins and laughter broke.

Radiant Farewell

Golden rays slip down,
Coconut boats sail by,
Laughter fills the air,
And seagulls start to fly.

Silly shadows stretch long,
As the sun waves goodbye,
Banana peels on the sand,
Oh, what a fruitcake sky!

Fruitful Skies

Splashes of yellow light,
Dancing on ocean waves,
Citrus giggles abound,
Where every laugh behaves.

Clouds wear fruity hats,
As the evening descends,
Jokes mix with the breeze,
And the day finally ends.

A Mosaic of Yellow

A drippy sun spills joy,
Painting the horizon bright,
Tropical giggles float,
In the warm, fading light.

Mangoes join the dance,
As the stars peek with glee,
Even the moon chuckles,
In this fruity jubilee.

Evening Glow in Paradise

Bouncing on the waves,
Silly dolphins dive and play,
Pineapple laughs at dusk,
As the sun turns to clay.

Every wave brings a grin,
As shadows start their prance,
In this glowing kingdom,
Where fruits learn how to dance.

Daylight's Last Kiss

The sun dips low, a golden prize,
As giggles echo, and humor flies.
Clouds dance bright, like silly clowns,
Painting giggles in velvet gowns.

Waves of light with a quirky twist,
"Chase the sun!" the critters insist.
With ice cream cones and sticky hands,
Laughter ripples across the lands.

The Golden Farewell

The day bows out with a wink and grin,
As shadows stretch and the night creeps in.
A rubber chicken floats up high,
Silly songs lift to the sky.

Cartwheeling clouds, they twist and spin,
Like joyful dancers at a whim.
With every hue, a jolly shout,
Who knew light could have so much clout?

Colors Dripping from the Sky

Splashing hues in a drunken spree,
Like paint splatters on a fun time spree.
The sky wears shades of root beer float,
With giggles rising, a jolly quote.

As the light leaks, a chuckle spills,
Filling hearts with playful thrills.
Marshmallow clouds in a bright cascade,
Making memories in this charade.

Euphoria in the Dimming Light

Crickets tune in, a comedic show,
As twilight glows, with a warm hello.
The horizon dresses in jellybean hues,
While the moon sneaks out in sparkly shoes.

With a laugh and a skip, the stars appear,
Avoiding the sun, they whisper cheer.
A parade of chuckles and dreams take flight,
Celebrating joy in the fading light.

Ambrosia at Dusk

The sky splashed yellow, a fruity delight,
A glow in the evening, oh what a sight!
With giggles and laughter, we feast on the hue,
A pudding of joy, for me and for you.

As clouds stretch like taffies, so sweet and so grand,
We chase down the flavors that life has planned.
With every bright shimmer, our spirits take flight,
And dance like the stars in the cool of the night.

Silhouetted Perfection

The palms strike a pose, in a sunset parade,
Twisting and turning, in fashion they swayed.
Like silhouettes frolicking, cheerful and spry,
A backdrop of waiting, the peachy-orange sky.

With shenanigans tossed in a tropical breeze,
We giggle at shadows, oh what a tease!
The horizon just chuckles, a canvas so bright,
Making us wonder, if this is delight.

Sweets Upon the Horizon

On the edge of the day, where the sweetness begins,
The sun splatters laughter, like candy-coated sins.
We raise up our glasses, to toast with a grin,
As flavors and colors make everyone win.

A carnival sky, with each splash and swirl,
We belly-laugh boldly, watch the world twirl.
With a wink from the dusk, and the mirth it provides,
We savor the sweetness, as the daylight hides.

Golden Tones of Tranquility

A golden embrace wraps around all in sight,
Dancing with chuckles, all day turns to night.
Truth be told, we giggle, at moments so fine,
While the sun winks and whispers, it's all quite divine.

With giggles and glee, we paint on the glow,
Sketching our dreams as the warm breezes flow.
Tranquility beams on this canvas of fun,
Where laughter and colors blend under one sun.

Soft Hues of the Evening Feast

The sky drips yellow, a glutton's delight,
Scattering laughter, in the fading light.
A fruit bowl giggles, full of bright cheer,
As dinner rolls by, we can't help but leer.

Twirling in twilight, we dance with glee,
Chasing the clouds like they're free jelly.
Silly conversations, with fruit on our face,
Even the moon breaks into a smile in this place.

Fruits and Fiery Skies

A citrus explosion, a sweet, zesty burst,
As fiery skies pop like candy, oh the thirst!
We juggle our snacks, and giggle in style,
While the sun throws tantrums, grinning all the while.

Glowing with laughter, the day wears its crown,
Dancing on rooftops, the whole town's a clown.
Adventures in hues, oh what a sight,
An orange giggle, then fades into night.

Luminescent Farewells

As light starts to fade, we waddle and sway,
Spilling our secrets in a bright, silly way.
Glowing hues linger, like jelly on toast,
While shadows play tag, we're goofier most.

Farewell to the sun, it gives us a wink,
Mixing giggles and juices in the drinks we clink.
The night is our canvas, we splash with delight,
Our laughter's the soundtrack as we dance into night.

A Whisper of Warmth

A warm chuckle gleams, as the day takes its bow,
The fireflies chuckle, not caring how.
In the glow of the dusk, we munch and we play,
Swapping our tales as the sun fades away.

With tummies like drums, we serenade the stars,
Belly laughs echo, and we climb to the bars.
A final warm hug from the day on the run,
We bid it adieu, oh what a fun one!

The Last Squeeze of Radiance

Golden rays slide down the sky,
Peeling laughter, oh my, oh my!
Splashes of giggles, bright and bold,
Turning twilight to vibrant gold.

Juicy dreams drip from the stars,
Delightful dances under Mars.
The day spills out in zesty cheer,
With every chuckle, night draws near.

Chasing Colors of Dusk

In the sky, colors twist and play,
What a comical end to the day!
Pinks and oranges, a riotous show,
Painting clouds, a wild glow.

On the horizon, a silly moon winks,
As the sunlight wobbles and sinks.
Laughter bubbles as stars drop in,
Gathering scrapes from the day's din.

Hues of Elysium

A riot of colors in evening's delight,
Frolicking hues in a playful fight.
Lavender clouds giggle and tease,
While the breeze dances with ease.

Cotton candy skies, sweet and fun,
Where everyone's dancing, and no one's won.
Jokes in the sunset, tangerine and more,
A comedy club at the ocean's shore.

Silken Skies and Sweet Fragrance

Silken skies wear a shimmering grin,
As twilight whispers where fun begins.
Scent of laughter in the air,
Twists and turns, without a care.

Fuzzy dreams plummet from heights,
Fruity puzzles in colorful flights.
As day clowns around, playing the fool,
Night dips in the sea, cool as a pool.

Ripening Hues of Sundown

The sky burst forth with yellow cheer,
As fruit flies danced, they brought a leer.
A hammock swayed with evening's praise,
While laughter echoed in sunset's gaze.

Flip-flops flung from sandy toes,
Sunbeams wrapped around like bees to flows.
The gentle breeze could not care less,
As we all embraced that fruity mess.

Clouds turned bright with citrus flair,
While seagulls squawked without a care.
Kids on the shore were painting dreams,
In shades of yellow, ripe with beams.

As daylight wanes, we seize the fun,
With chuckles shared 'neath the glowing sun.
Our giggles mix with a fruity zest,
In the grand game of smiles, we are blessed.

Citrus Glow Beneath the Horizon

A slice of sun dips low and bright,
With flavors bold and pure delight.
The world awash in vibrant cheer,
As friends toast cups of juice near.

Lemonade stands like candy stalls,
Where laughter bubbles, and fun just sprawls.
We chase the colors, twirl and play,
With a citrus glow to end the day.

In the distance, a beach ball flies,
Bouncing high beneath orange skies.
We giggle at the clumsiness
That comes from walking in beachy mess.

As shadows stretch, we dance and sing,
Our silly moves a joyful fling.
This funny time beneath the sun,
Is an evening that won't be outdone.

The Last Gleam of Day

The sky explodes with shades of glee,
A vibrant show, so wild and free.
Every burst makes the painters sigh,
As goofy clouds drift and float by.

Sunglasses on, we must confess,
Our fashion sense is quite the mess.
A picnic spread with snacks galore,
And sandwiches that we can't ignore.

Footprints traced in golden sand,
Turn into laughter—oh, isn't it grand?
A sunset party, we're feeling bold,
With tales of victories, bright and old.

As daylight fades, we raise a cheer,
For every silly laugh we hold dear.
In this last gleam, we find our way,
Transforming moments into play.

Sun-Kissed Whispers

A playful breeze through palm trees sways,
As sunlight wraps us in golden rays.
With sun-kissed cheeks and gleeful grins,
The day begins where laughter spins.

We tell tall tales of giant fruit,
While gnawing on our snacky loot.
Our whispers twinkle like stars at night,
In the warm embrace of fading light.

Chocolate stains and sticky hands,
Crafting castles on the sands.
With every giggle, joy takes flight,
As sunset comes and seals the night.

So here we gather, carefree and bold,
To share a laugh or story told.
With sun-kissed whispers in the air,
Adventures linger everywhere.

Golden Horizons

The sky's a bright yellow, oh what a sight,
A giant fruit shows up, just after light.
Chasing birds with laughter, it glows so bold,
As shadows stretch out, tales of fun unfold.

Kites made of laughter swoop and dance,
While monkeys juggle joy, given half a chance.
The sun's a slippery jokester, that's quite clear,
As it brightens the beach and all the cheer.

Twilight Tropics

Evening brings giggles with a tangerine twist,
Where palms sway and play, you can't resist.
The horizon blushes, like a prankster's grin,
As the day bids farewell and fun begins.

Sandcastles topple, as waves play their game,
With sand between toes, no one feels shame.
The sun takes a bow, a clown till the end,
Leaving behind chuckles, as daylight descends.

Citrus Dreams at Dusk

When dusk rolls around, we have a fling,
With citrusy scents and dancing spring.
The purple and orange twirl in delight,
As giggles erupt in the soft fading light.

A hammock swings low, inviting a smile,
While critters tell stories, in their own style.
A fruit basket spills, laughter takes flight,
In dreams where the silly meets warm twilight.

The Last Peel of Day

At the edge of the world, the day takes a dip,
Peeling away colors, like a cheeky trip.
A wink from the sun, as it starts to hide,
Wrapping the sea in golden slide.

Backyard barbecues with friends on a roll,
Flipping sausages, aiming for the pole.
The sun slips away, a giggle in its wake,
Leaving behind a world that dances and shakes.

Skyborne Banquets

In a fruit bowl sky, we dine,
Floating snacks on clouds divine,
Peeling laughter from the air,
Banqueting without a care.

Custard clouds in splendid swirls,
Giggling feathers, laughing curls,
Harvest skies with silly treats,
Bananas dance on breezy beats.

Tropical breezes serve the zest,
Silly guests decide the rest,
Sunshine slips a wink our way,
As we snack and dance away.

Golden drips of joyy arise,
With silly shades that mesmerize,
Feasting warmth in dusk's embrace,
Fruits and fun set every pace.

Warm Embrace of Dusk

As daylight dips in fruity bliss,
The world enjoys a tangy kiss,
Warm hugs from the sun's last rays,
Jokes are shared in sunset plays.

Silly shadows start to roam,
Chasing giggles, feeling home,
Underneath the lavender sky,
Toast to twilight, giggle high!

Whispers dance on breezy turns,
While laughter in the evening burns,
With fruits that twinkle, gleeful tease,
In the dusk where we find ease.

A Juicy Goodbye

As day waves hello to the night,
We wave back with fruity delight,
Saying cheerio to the sun,
And on this ride, we just have fun.

The orange sky does giggle back,
As nutty clouds begin to crack,
Slicing time with hearty glee,
In this juicy jubilee!

With every glimmer, flavors blend,
Bidding dusk a merry send,
Juicy tales and laughter gleam,
As we slip into twilight's dream.

Melodies of the Setting Sun

A serenade from skies of art,
With silly tunes that shake the heart,
Strumming chords of amber light,
As shadows start their funny flight.

Notes of gold in breezes play,
Nature's band starts up the sway,
Tropical laughter fills the air,
While the sun spins on a dare.

In this concert, we all sway,
With giggles leading every way,
Bantering with the fading sun,
As the day declares we've won!

Warm Embrace of Dusk

The sky slips on a yellow hat,
As clouds wear shades, how about that?
Laughter bubbles with the sun's last gleam,
Day's ending feels like a silly dream.

Silly shadows dance with glee,
On this twilight stage, wild and free.
Even the crickets hum along,
To the tune of a sunset song.

With splashes of gold in every beam,
It's a sunset party, or so it seems!
All the palm trees twist and sway,
In this funny, goofy, bright display.

Sundrenched Dreams

The sun dives into a playful swirl,
While colors frolic, twist, and twirl.
Pineapple hats atop heads so bright,
As day bids farewell and night takes flight.

Dreams of coconuts start to float,
On waves of giggles, look at that boat!
A crab plays chess with a cheeky seagull,
In this quirky twilight, we all feel full.

Frolicking stars can't help but prance,
Joining the dusk in a wild dance.
With every ray, a chuckle grows,
In this sundrenched dream, anything goes.

Palette of Paradise

Brush strokes of orange paint the sky,
While flamingos watch as day slips by.
A toucan wheels in a comedic flight,
Adding laughter to the vibrant sight.

Palm trees giggle, their leaves a-flutter,
As the sun drops in a splash of butter.
Jellybean clouds float on high,
Making wishes as they drift by.

Barrels of monkeys swing with flair,
Chasing each other without a care.
In every color, slightly absurd,
Nature's jokes are easily heard.

Glowing Tropics

The sun sprinkles gold like confetti sweet,
As the day bids farewell, can't be beat!
With laughter bubbling like fizzy drinks,
Tropical fun is what everyone thinks.

Coconuts giggle in the breeze,
As seagulls plot shenanigans with ease.
A turtle in shades makes quite a scene,
Strutting his stuff, looking quite keen.

The horizon glows like a glowing pop,
With colors that bounce, skip, and hop.
In these glowing tropics, all feels right,
As day turns to night, igniting delight.

The Warmth of Sugary Skies

When the sun slips low in the sky,
The clouds wear a smile, oh my!
Peanut butter dreams float near,
As jellyfish laugh, what a cheer!

Marshmallows dance on golden rays,
Wiggling joy in a syrupy haze.
Pies fly by like happy birds,
Chirping out the silliest words!

Kites made of cookie crumble,
Swirling like a giggling rumble.
In this land of sweet delight,
Laughter echoes into the night!

So grab a spoon and take a seat,
As sunlight turns our day to treat!
With sugary skies above our heads,
Let's leap like jelly, see where it leads!

Luminous Spheres at Twilight

Twinkling like disco balls high,
The stars begin their silly fly.
Juggling planets catch the breeze,
While comets trip with utmost ease.

The moon wears shades, cool and bright,
Grooving under shimmering light.
Clouds play tag, loopy and bold,
Tickling cheeks, a sight to behold!

Cactus might twirl, who knows?
Mango trees do silly pros.
In a sky of swirly snacks,
We slide on rainbows, never slack!

Giggles echo from the ground,
As we toss pebbles all around.
With luminous spheres up high,
Join the fun, don't be shy!

Vibrant Currents of Light

Dancing beams in delightful blend,
Spinning joy that seems to transcend.
Cotton candy clouds drift by,
With lollipops bursting in the sky!

Rivers of honey flow and swirl,
As the tickled daylight twirls.
Peaches glow in the sunset's glow,
Creating a sweet and lively show!

Fireflies buzz with laughter bright,
Filling the air with pure delight.
Jellybeans plop on the floor,
Only to bounce and scream for more!

With vibrant currents, we partake,
In a carnival of silly shake.
Let's welcome dusk with every bite,
Where sweetness dances with the night!

Sweet Serenities of Evening

Evening falls with a giggle loud,
Peanut shells kick, they're so proud.
Taffy trees sway in the breeze,
With poppy seeds doing the tease!

The moon takes selfies on its phone,
While crickets dance and hum their tone.
Chocolate rivers flow with glee,
Inviting all for a tasty spree!

Sprinkled stars begin to shout,
As gummy bears jump all about.
With a wink, the sun bids adieu,
Leaving happiness in golden hue!

So let us revel in this night,
Where silly dreams take their flight.
With sweet serenities around,
In laughter's arms, we're tightly bound!

Dreams in Tropical Colors

In a world of yellow hues,
Monkeys dance in shades of blues.
Floating on a leaf so bright,
They giggle under twinkling light.

Cotton candy clouds above,
Swaying like a lover's glove.
Tickling breezes start to play,
Turning night into a sway.

Twists and loops in vibrant glow,
Sipping drinks with joy to show.
Chasing silly shadows near,
Where laughter spreads like summer cheer.

The Sun's Waving Goodbye

The sun dips low with a silly grin,
Trying on a shade of skin.
A wink and nod as it does leap,
Into the ocean's arms so deep.

Cocktails spill with giggles loud,
As the sun becomes the crowd.
Lay back and let the colors melt,
A cozy warmth that's always felt.

Chasing rays like kittens bum,
Tickling waves with a little drum.
The horizon sways, makes a scene,
Where silly dreams queue up to glean.

Hints of Sunshine in the Twilight

Twilight paints with strokes of fun,
Color bursts, a lively run.
Glowing fruits on every tree,
Sing a tune of jubilee.

Bright fires flicker, skies like jam,
Bouncing ballads, oh what a slam!
The stars all giggle, twinkle bright,
Waiting for the moon's delight.

A dance of flavors, warm and sweet,
With laughter making summer heat.
Silly shimmers in the breeze,
A playful spirit, teasing trees.

Ripe Skies

The sky is ripe, like fruit on trees,
Sprinkled laughter floats with ease.
Jokester clouds begin to tease,
Sharing giggles with the bees.

Every sunset wears a crown,
Painting cheeks of pink and brown.
Fireflies join the evening's song,
Dancing where the stars belong.

Coconut whispers in the air,
Tickling senses, beyond compare.
As shadows play in sunset's grace,
We're all just kids in a big embrace.

A Vibrant Symphony of Colors

Golden glow spills from the sky,
Like liquid laughter, oh so spry.
Clouds wear shades of fruity pride,
As evening giggles play and slide.

Juicy hues dance on the breeze,
Tickling toes and swaying knees.
The sun slips down with cheeky flair,
A wink that floats on evening air.

Sassy rays sizzle, pop, and bloom,
Transforming twilight into a room.
With citrus whispers, night takes wing,
And stars join in the jazzy swing.

So let us toast this wacky sight,
Where colors clash and hearts feel light.
In this rainbow, we all belong,
Underneath the sunset's song.

The Fruitful Goodbye

A fruity farewell drips with cheer,
As daylight fades, the night draws near.
Lemonade skies just can't resist,
Sipping up the sunset's twist.

The sun yawns wide, a ripping grin,
As fruity dreams start to begin.
With giggles wrapped in golden hues,
The sky dons sparkles like confetti, too.

It's a party on the horizon line,
Balloons of color, all so fine.
Farewell to the day with a silly hat,
As the twilight interacts with a sprightly chat.

With each wink from the fading light,
The day plays coy, tucked in the night.
We'll wave goodbye, but not for long,
As tomorrow sings its vibrant song.

Dusk's Tropical Reverie

A joking dusk with laughter spills,
Painting waves with sunset thrills.
Coconuts dance on ocean's crest,
As colors riff in a playful jest.

Topping the day with frozen glee,
Mango sorbet, wild and free.
The horizon chuckles, it's quite a sight,
As day blends into a caramel night.

Jellyfish float in the shimmering tide,
As jellybeans giggle, side by side.
With every hue, a punchline falls,
In this pastel clown, nature calls.

The world basks in sweet, golden jest,
As the sun drapes warmth—a comfy vest.
So let's revel in this cheeky show,
Where colors amuse and good vibes flow.

Embrace of Color and Warmth

A splash of sunshine, a sprinkle of cheer,
As day takes its bow, the night draws near.
Colors collide in laughter's embrace,
As the sky wears a jubilant face.

With tangerine giggles bouncing high,
Each giggly cloud floats by and sighs.
Peachy whispers entwine together,
An uproar of joy in the golden tether.

Painting shadows that skip and leap,
The fruit-filled hues in harmony sweep.
As chortles burst like a piñata's grin,
In this comical dance, we all spin.

So let the sky tease with playful sight,
In colors that urge us to feel just right.
With warmth surrounding, laughter in tow,
Together we'll glow, as friendships flow.

Enchantment of the Setting Sun

Golden glow spills across the sky,
As fruit flies by, and we all sigh.
A dance of yellow, ripe and bright,
We laugh at shadows, what a sight!

With playful hues that tease our eyes,
Like silly jokes in sunset skies.
We chase the rays, a zany crew,
In the warm light of the evening hue.

The giggles bounce like bouncing balls,
As evening drapes its color calls.
We snap our photos, strike a pose,
In fruity vibes, the laughter grows.

As twilight whispers, "Let's have fun!"
We crown ourselves the golden one.
With silly hats and wacky glee,
We toast to joy, just you and me.

Vibrant Farewells

The day departs with vibrant flair,
Like smushed fruit in a worn-out chair.
We wave goodbye to sunburned rays,
And joke about our golden days.

With sugary whispers in the air,
We share inside jokes without a care.
The sky's a canvas, splashed and bright,
We giggle softly at the sight.

As the horizon shows its best,
We throw a party, never rest.
With fruit-themed songs that make us grin,
Who knew the fun would never thin?

Each splash of color gets a cheer,
As if the sun says, "Come right here!"
We dance like crazy, run and play,
In the warm glow, we laugh away.

Where Sweetness Meets the Sky

A citrus splash brightens the scene,
As laughter bubbles up between.
We spot the clouds like fluffy treats,
And skip along in sugary beats.

The evening soars on zany wings,
With jokes that swirl like wild swings.
In twilight's arms, we leap and hop,
Reflecting light, we never stop.

We mix up colors, what a show!
Like candies tossed in a bright rainbow.
We chase the twilight with a grin,
In treasure hunts of where we've been.

With every giggle, the sky's aglow,
Our playful spirits, wildly flow.
As sunset melts into our hearts,
We claim this magic; never parts.

The Last Splash of Citrus

As daylight fades, we raise a cheer,
With zesty laughter, never fear.
The sky's a joke, with colors bright,
Each splash of citrus feels so right.

With silly games, we run amok,
And share some quirks like a funny clock.
With fruity dreams and evening's tease,
We dance around like buzzing bees.

The sun makes faces, we poke and play,
In the playful light of the ending day.
The sky drips sweetness, we dive right in,
In golden giggles, we spin and spin.

As the horizon swallows the sun's last gleam,
We savor moments, laugh and dream.
In this fruity finale, we all unite,
With hearts as bright as the starry night.

Melodies of the Dimiing Sun

As the sky dons its fruity attire,
Laughter bursts like juice from a tire.
Clouds dance in hues of bright yellow,
Even the birds sing like a jello!

Goofy shadows stretch and sway,
While crickets tune in to play.
The day flips like a pancake round,
In this feast where joy is found.

Giggling beams beam down from above,
Even the squirrels are in love.
Silly skies all swirled in cheer,
Capturing smiles for all to share.

With a wink, the sun starts to tease,
Whispers of fun in the evening breeze.
As the day stumbles into night,
We dance in the glow, feeling light!

Radiant Spheres and Golden Tones

Round and shiny, like a treat,
The sun prances on its feet.
Wobbling clouds join in the fun,
As twilight giggles at everyone.

Blushing rays paint creatures tall,
While tossing shadows like a ball.
A sprinkle of orange, a dash of peach,
It's the kind of day you can't quite reach!

Laughter echoes through the air,
As sunset spills its fruity flair.
Bring the punch to make it bright,
In this joyous, glowing light!

Friends gather to toast the sight,
Gold-infused hearts feel so light.
With every giggle, nature plays,
Welcome, silly end to our days!

Sweet Silhouettes at Sunset

Figures waltz against the glow,
Spinning tales in sunset's flow.
The horizon blushes, it can't deny,
Silly antics under a fruit-flavored sky.

With the sun doing limbo low,
Even the trees lean to and fro.
Butterflies sport a golden hue,
Laughing along in this evening view.

Kids giggle as they chase a light,
Shadows stretching, what a sight!
Chasing dreams on this juicy stage,
The day bows out with a cheeky page.

All the world wraps in a wink,
As colors blend, the world starts to sink.
Every moment drips with delight,
Savoring the playfulness of night!

Juicy Reflections of the Day

Peeking through the golden trees,
A juicy smile floats in the breeze.
Dancing light with a cherry twist,
How could anyone resist?

The sun slips down, an orange slice,
Belly laughs echo, oh so nice!
Frogs leap by in silly tune,
Shaking hands with the rising moon.

Splash of crimson, a hint of fun,
Even the shadows start to run.
Hilarious moments we can't forget,
Reflected in this flavor set!

With giggles ringing in the air,
Sunset hugs without a care.
Plucking joys from golden beams,
Chasing laughter, chasing dreams!

Reflections in the Golden Hour

In the sky, a yellow splash,
Clouds dance in a fruity bash.
Giggling rays of playful light,
Chasing shadows, blurring sight.

Palm trees sway with a silly grin,
Tickling breezes on my skin.
Sunbeams juggle through the air,
Making me forget all care.

Laughter ripples on the sea,
Waves whisper secrets just for me.
As the day begins to fade,
I chuckle at this wacky parade.

With every twirl, the colors blend,
Nature's humor knows no end.
In this hour of golden play,
I'll forever wish to stay.

Sunkissed Tropics

In a land of yellow bliss,
Every mango dreams of this.
Dancing shadows on the ground,
Chasing smiles that bounce around.

Coconuts wear tiny hats,
As crabs perform their silly chats.
Laughter echoes through the trees,
Carried gently by the breeze.

Every sunset sings a tune,
Whispered secrets to the moon.
Underneath the vibrant glow,
Even fish have fun, you know!

On the shore, the colors play,
Fruits and sunsets have their say.
In this tropic, bright and bold,
Funny stories will be told.

When Light Bends

As the light begins to bend,
Twisting tales without an end.
A marigold monkey swings around,
Tickling rays on the ground.

Frog in shades does a hip hop,
Dancing algae, never stop.
Everything glows in golden cheer,
With a nighttime hug so near.

Oh, the hues, a quirky feast,
Even clouds turn to a beast.
With a wink, the sunlight strays,
While nature giggles in the rays.

Spinning, twirling, what a sight,
The world plays tricks in the light.
As the sky begins to fade,
I laugh at this merry charade.

The Lush Light of Twilight

In the twilight's cheeky glow,
The world sparks with a show.
Lemons throw a party bright,
Juggling stars with sheer delight.

Pineapples wear their sunny shades,
As night starts to invade.
Silly shadows paint the ground,
While giggles echo all around.

Twinkling stars join the dance,
Causing fruits to take a chance.
With every burst of laughter shared,
Nature's joy is proudly declared.

In this lush, enchanted hour,
Life blooms with a fruity power.
As the colors slowly blend,
Funny memories never end.

A Bounty of Evening Colors

The skies are splashed with yellow hue,
Like fruit salads, fresh and new.
Cotton candy clouds float with glee,
As critters dance around the tree.

Pineapples wear their sun hat bright,
While squirrels giggle in delight.
Alligators in shades so bold,
Laugh at stories that they told.

The juice falls down with every drip,
A sunset smoothie, take a sip!
Skaters glide on orange beams,
As the world drips with silly dreams.

With such a feast for all to see,
The evening giggles play with glee.
Cartwheel stars then light the way,
In flavors of the end of day.

Harvest Moon on the Horizon

A grinning moon peeks from the side,
Like a playful wolf on a joyride.
The stars all twinkle, wink, and blink,
In light so sweet, it makes you think.

Pumpkins roll, their laughter sell,
Each one telling tales so swell.
Goblins swarm with fruited cheer,
Singing songs you want to hear.

Cornfields dance in evening light,
As fireflies take their joyful flight.
The night is ripe with fruity fun,
As dreams are served, one by one.

What a feast of sights and sounds,
Where silly chaos joyfully abounds.
And though the moon may have its say,
Tomorrow's plot will start the play.

Where Day Meets Night

The sun slips down with a rosy glow,
Like a sleepy kid put on show.
Lemons laugh, they squeeze with zest,
Chasing twilight in a jest.

Cherries giggle, rolls on grass,
While shadows grow, they whisper, 'Pass!'
The day and night high-five with flair,
A fruit parade; mishaps everywhere!

Pineapples skate, their tops all fight,
In a race to welcome in the night.
Blueberries tangle in twilight steep,
While juicy wishes begin to creep.

But as the stars take their sweet place,
The sun grins wide, a cheeky face.
On this stage where light is bright,
Mirth unfolds in playful flight.

Mango Melodies at Sundown

With every sunset's golden sheen,
The mango sings, a fruity queen.
Strumming vines, a joyful tune,
As the day melts into moon.

Papayas sway in rhyming lines,
Stirring up the sweet designs.
Ripe laughter drips from every tree,
In a cabaret for you and me.

Lime and lemon spin a jig,
As nectarines dance big and big.
The evening's filled with fruity chatter,
As all the colors swirl and splatter.

Oh, come and taste this juicy joy,
A feast of laughter none can destroy.
On this stage, the fruits unite,
For cheeky fun, till morning light.

The Fruitful Horizon

On the edge where laughter spills,
Where ripe folks climb up the hills,
Yellow skies make toast with cheer,
As fruity giggles fill the sphere.

In every cloud a smoothie blend,
A punchline waiting for a friend,
With jests fruity as they sway,
The horizon wears its bright bouquet.

The sun squishes like a peach,
Its glow is silly, oh, what a reach!
As chuckles bounce like balls on ground,
A parade of fruit is all around.

So here we toast this funny sight,
Where veggies dare to frolic in light,
In this world where sunlight jives,
The horizon laughs, and joy thrives.

When Day Sips Night

As night approaches, day takes a sip,
Of twilight's nectar, sweet on the lip,
The moon laughs, a silvery grin,
While stars wear hats, glimmering thin.

Colors blend, a fruity cocktail,
With giggles bouncing up the trail,
The sun winks, wearing shades so bright,
As shadows dance, inviting the night.

Lemon and lime light the dusk,
A zesty breeze, a playful musk,
Each cheeky star, a wink in disguise,
Sipping on laughter, under sky pies.

In this moment, hilarity reigns,
Where day meets night and joy entertains,
So raise your glass to the sky so wide,
Where fun spills over like a wild ride.

Joyful Horizons of Ambrosial Light

In skies soaked with citrus delight,
Where laughter bubbles, taking flight,
Horizon's edge flirts with orange glee,
As fruity dreams dance, wild and free.

The day giggles, a prankster bold,
With tangerine tales waiting to be told,
Each ray of sunshine wears a grin,
Inviting all mischief to begin.

Pineapple clouds frolic in the breeze,
A merry chase, just like the bees,
With every hue a ticklish tease,
Joyful horizons sway with ease.

Embrace this light, so cozy and sweet,
Where silliness and sunshine meet,
A delightful patch where humor blooms,
In ambrosial light, all sadness zooms.

Evening's Coral Embrace

In a coral glow, the day unfolds,
Where laughter's warmth is joyfully told,
The sun tucks in with a fruity grin,
As silliness wraps the world akin.

With cartoonish clouds, colors collide,
A riot of hues take a rollercoaster ride,
Orange and pink with tender delight,
Whispering secrets to the shimmering night.

The stars giggle, twinkling so bright,
Gossiping tales of the goofy light,
As the moon peeks, a jester's applause,
Celebrating humor without a pause.

So dance in the glow of this silly dusk,
Where giggles bubble like fruity musk,
In evening's coral, embrace the mirth,
A jubilant life, a whimsical earth.

Sunset Serenade

The sky's a split banana, oh what a sight,
As colors dance and play, in pure delight.
Chasing goofy clouds, with laughter loud,
A silly serenade, makes us all proud.

The sun, a yellow jester, takes its bow,
With fruit-shaped beams, it shows us how.
Waves of giggles wash upon the shore,
In this twilight show, who could ask for more?

Bright shades of whimsy, dreams take to flight,
Painting our hearts with strokes of light.
Jokes echo through palm trees, fluttering free,
In this golden hour, it's just you and me.

An evening symphony, each hue a tune,
Beneath the glowing orb, we'll dance till noon.
Curling up with laughter, as the day takes a run,
In our sunset paradise, we all become One.

The Lure of Tropical Light

A peeler in the sky, oh so bright,
Twists and turns in the fading light.
With every shade, we giggle with glee,
This fruity allure is calling to me.

Laughter floats, like a breeze from the sea,
Tickling the waves, come dance with me.
Each glance at the horizon steals my breath,
In this hilarity, we are born afresh.

Silly shadows bounce, like kids in a game,
Entwined in colors, never quite the same.
With ice cream mustaches, we run hand in hand,
At the edge of the day, laughter's our band.

Underneath the twilight, stories ignite,
As we twirl in the glow, what a sight!
Our lives painted lightly by the sun's warm kiss,
These joyful moments, we'd never miss.

Caramel Hues of Evening

Swirls of caramel dance in the air,
Snickering at clouds, without a care.
In the gentle brush of the day's end glow,
Where chuckles collide, and breezes blow.

Hues of honey, dripping with cheer,
Make everything seem more fun when near.
A splash of laughter, a sprinkle of light,
Gather 'round cozy, as day turns to night.

Silly shadows stretch, they twist and bend,
In this vibrant sketch, let the fun never end.
With the sun's cheeky wink, as it takes its leave,
We toast to the twilight, in jest, we believe.

Caught in the glow, we jest and we play,
As colors confide in the fading day.
Sweet caramel moments, wrapped tight like a hug,
In the warmth of laughter, to the night we'll plug.

Sunkissed Yellow Wonders

Oh, look at the sky, a golden surprise,
Bouncing bright light from dusk's warm eyes.
Splashes of laughter, as bright as the sun,
In this wild wonder, we are all one.

With giggles and cheer, we chase the rays,
Each twilight twinkle in a silly craze.
The horizon grins back, in hues of cheer,
As we bask in the glow of this funny frontier.

The sun drips laughter, in vibrant streams,
Each sunset tells stories wrapped up in dreams.
With friends all around, it's a jubilant blast,
We'll laugh at the shadows that swiftly cast.

In this joyous world, we leap and we prance,
Underneath glowing skies, we twirl and dance.
So here's to the magic, the smiles, and the fun,
In the hues of the evening, we shine like the sun.

Melting Horizons

On the edge of the world where the sun likes to slide,
Colors drip down like a gooey fruit tide.
Strawberry and mango paint the sea bright,
As we giggle and munch on snacks, what a sight!

Clouds wear pajamas, fluffy and round,
Chasing the daylight, they tumble and bound.
With a wink and a flick, the horizon shakes,
Whimsical shadows with wide, goofy grins make.

The seagulls are dancing, they join in the fun,
Especially the one that thinks it can run.
With feet made of jelly and wings made of cheese,
It flops in the sunset, bringing us to our knees!

So here in this place where the light likes to play,
Even the jellyfish giggle and sway.
We sip our drinks while the world starts to melt,
And bubbles of laughter are perfectly felt.

Tropical Twilight

As evening approaches, the sky starts to grin,
A pineapple hat is twirling, oh what a win!
Lemon-lime laughter in the twilight air,
Making shadows dance without a single care.

Coconuts chuckle from their lofty old trees,
While the breeze tells jokes that tickle the knees.
Stars pop out like candy, one by one,
Singing the praises of a day full of fun.

The ocean's a mirror of giggles and light,
Wobbling fish join the party tonight.
With glittering scales, they shimmy and sway,
While we splash about in a ridiculous way!

As the sun winks goodbye with a warm orange bow,
We munch on the day's fruits, all juicy and wow!
Together we laugh as the dusk settles down,
In this tropical twilight, we wear our crown.

Golden Skies at Dusk

The sun's like a joke that's just too sublime,
It rolls off the horizon, having a good time.
With tangerine giggles, it bids us farewell,
As fruity illusions start to rebel.

Clouds play hopscotch in purple and gold,
Making antics outrageous, adventures unfold.
While shadows get stretched, like rubbery gloves,
We frolic and fumble, feeling the love.

Citrus-flavored whispers float through the air,
Tickling our senses without a care.
We caper around like we're lost on a spree,
Finding joy in the light, so wild and free!

As the world takes a bow in the twilight's embrace,
We feast on laughter, a delicious taste.
With each silly moment, the fun multiplies,
In this golden spectacle that paints our skies.

The Fruit of Evening Light

When the sky starts to giggle, the fruit comes alive,
Lemons and cherries dance, they jive!
A festival of colors, like candy and cream,
As we munch on delight, caught in a dream.

The horizon spills juice, oh what a mess!
Kiwis and oranges, we say yes, yes, yes!
They slip and they slide in a slippery race,
Creating our laughter, in this vibrant space.

Bouncing through twilight, the fruit parties hard,
Grapes in sunglasses, striking a pose in the yard.
We join in the frolic, our giggles collide,
With every burst of flavor, used as our guide.

So in this sweet moment, we relish the night,
When even the fruit finds a way to delight.
Together we play, under skies full of bliss,
In this joyful embrace, how could we miss?

The Aura of Dimming Day

As the light starts to fade, birds put on a show,
Chasing shadows and giggles, with nowhere to go.
The sky's a big canvas, painted in cheer,
Where clowns on the horizon lift spirits, oh dear!

Lemonade sips and the sun's final bow,
Stretchy shadows dance, what's happening now?
Pies on the window, watching the flare,
Like a juggling act, with flair to spare!

The rollercoaster winds, laughter in the breeze,
Clouds tossing confetti, in colors that tease.
Tickles of twilight and a wink from the moon,
The day isn't done; it still has its tune!

In a world of sweet chaos, we twirl and we spin,
Dreaming of adventures, let the giggles begin!
Hold on to the fun as the day takes its last,
With a silly parade, we leave nothing unpassed.

Sweet Light Farewell

The sky drips with orange, a dessert on a plate,
Silly shadows appear, they can't seem to wait.
A great monster sun yawns, stretching wide with a grin,
While bored little stars wonder just where to begin.

Cotton candy clouds float, having too much fun,
Balloons of all colors dance just for the sun.
A giggle once spoken, now echoes through night,
As owls play charades, oh what a sight!

The grass joins the party, tickling bare feet,
Crickets start clapping, keeping the beat.
Glowing fireflies weave tales in the air,
With whispers of mischief, a playful affair.

So let's raise our cups, toast to the sky,
As daylight drifts off, with a wink, oh my!
Tonight our festivity, unique and bright,
Shall hum with the laughter of pure, silly light!

The Golden Embrace of Twilight

The sun bows low, like a funny old chap,
Juggling its rays while taking a nap.
Peeking through curtains of dimming delight,
It tickles the clouds, oh what a sight!

Marshmallow puffs squish down for a hug,
As bright pink straws poke at the evening's mug.
Everyone's laughing, make room for the jest,
In the glow of the twilight, we take off our vests!

The day whispers secrets to the giggling trees,
With a tickle of laughter rustling the leaves.
Fireflies come out, trying to join in,
With flashes of mischief, like zany kin!

Soft melodies swirl, tickling the air,
As the sun's golden embrace catches us unaware.
So, let the moon giggle and start the night's play,
Chasing the drowsiness of bright sunny day!

Evening's Taste of Wonder

Crisp popcorn skies, with promises galore,
Golden giggles echo, who could ask for more?
Marigold smiles stretch wide at the sight,
Painting a portrait of pure delight!

Hiccups of laughter bounce high up in flight,
While the shadows tell stories in the deepening night.
The fireflies serve sparkles like confetti in cheer,
As the moon plays the hero, bringing us near!

Each star a wink, with secrets in tow,
Welcoming mayhem, while twilight will glow.
A silly parade of whims takes its time,
Riding on dreams, in rhythm and rhyme.

Let's dance on the grass, chase away all our cares,
For evening's full promise is fun everywhere!
With a pinch of wonder, we'll jump into play,
As the world turns around, we'll laugh all the way!

The Enchantment of Dusk

In skies so ripe with yellow glow,
The sun slips down, a clumsy show.
A giggle bursts from clouds above,
As nature laughs, it's time for love.

Fruits wear crowns of golden hue,
Dancing beams, they twirl anew.
Chasing laughter on the breeze,
While shadows hide behind the trees.

As daylight bids its silly cheer,
The evening whispers, 'Don't fear here!'
Echoes of giggles in the air,
Softly strummed on sunshine's hair.

With every wink, the sky exclaims,
'Join the fun, forget the games!'
So bonkers bright, the twilight beams,
Wrap us up in silly dreams.

Tropical Echoes

The sky erupts in fruity sights,
As giggles dance on tropical nights.
A beach ball rolls where shadows play,
Chasing mischief 'til the day.

Hammocks swing with laughter's tune,
As palms sway gently, like a boon.
The echo of nonsense fills the air,
A cheeky spark that's always there.

Sunset dips like chocolate fondue,
While flip-flops skip on skies so blue.
Each burst of color makes us grin,
As the day melts like an ice-cold skin.

With fruity drinks in every hand,
We toast to peace in this wild land.
The laughter flows and waves collide,
In this parody where dreams abide.

Where Light Meets Flavor

The horizon glows with tangy fun,
Our giggles burst like bubbles spun.
Lemonade skies, and laughter light,
Mix flavors bright with pure delight.

Pineapples joke with the coconut trees,
As fireflies play tag with the breeze.
The taste of joy drips from the sun,
Packing flavor in every pun.

Clouds wear hats of whipped cream white,
While we catch dreams in fading light.
Each laugh a splash of flavor sweet,
As day gives way to night's heartbeat.

The fruit parade of colors gleams,
Where giggles flow like silly streams.
We feast on twilight's playful flair,
In this feast that we all share.

The Dance of Dusk

Twilight twirls in a fruity dress,
The sky's a canvas, chaos, no less.
Wiggling stars start their playful tease,
As night unfolds with giggles and ease.

Whimsical lights take center stage,
While shadows leap like a playful page.
Each breeze a joke we cannot tell,
As laughter ripples like a sweet shell.

The moon winks down, a jester grand,
Splashing smiles across the land.
With every chuckle the day departs,
Leaving sparkles in our hearts.

So let's embrace this dusky sight,
Join the dance of day and night.
In colors flung with silly flair,
We'll spin in joy, without a care.

A Dance of Color and Light

In the sky, a splash of yellow,
Clouds giggle, looking quite mellow.
The sun slips down, a clown in disguise,
Painting the world with fruity goodbyes.

Laughter echoes in the cooling breeze,
As daylight bows with such playful ease.
A dance so bright, it makes one grin,
Who knew the sky could be so akin?

Lighthearted hues swirl all around,
Chasing shadows from the ground.
A wink and nod, the sun takes flight,
Stepping down from its playful height.

So here we sit, with drinks in hand,
Watching this show, so wonderfully planned.
As colors collide, we cheer and jest,
In this silly light, we feel truly blessed.

Fruits of the Flaming Sky

Citrus splashes, bold and bright,
The sky a canvas, what a sight!
Juicy laughter mix with rays,
As nighttime tiptoes, in fun-filled ways.

Flaming oranges and kiwi dreams,
The sunset crackles, or so it seems.
A giggle from the horizon's kiss,
What a fruity spectacle, we can't resist!

With hearts aflutter, we join the cheer,
Each color bursts like a berry in beer.
As the sun teases, it waves goodbye,
We promise to return, oh my, oh my!

Who wouldn't forget such a playful glance,
In a world where colors in the sky dance?
With friends nearby, the laughter stays,
As the sky performs this tasty ballet!

In the Glow of Tropical Flare

The sun's a fruit salad, zesty and bright,
Sprinkling laughter, what a delight!
Tropical tones flare with glee,
As day tips its hat, night's jubilee.

Golden rays twist, a playful parade,
With each sunset wonder, we are serenade.
A lighthearted show, we all applaud,
As the sky breathes fire, it seems so flawed!

In this glowing aura, smiles ignite,
Each shade a sweet treat, a whimsical sight.
Snickers glide on warm evening air,
As the sun retires without a care.

Buzzing with joy, we dance in sway,
As flavors of laughter steal us away.
In this vibrant picture, life's a big tease,
With tropical hues, we float on a breeze!

Warm Embrace of a Leisurely Evening

The sun dips low, a golden hug,
Wrapping the world in a citrus rug.
Laughter spills like juice from above,
As the sky dons its glow of love.

Beneath the warmth, we lounge and jest,
Finding joy in the day's playful quest.
Each orange blush and cherry flare,
Sends waves of giggles floating in air.

With friends surrounding, bursts of cheer,
Moments like this, we hold so dear.
The sun winks down, oh what a tease,
Painting the evening with fruity ease.

So we toast to the sky, in all its hues,
With punchlines and dreams, nothing to lose.
In this jovial realm, our spirits lift,
As we bask in the twilight's delicious gift.

www.ingramcontent.com/pod-product-compliance
Lightning Source LLC
Chambersburg PA
CBHW070004300426
43661CB00141B/218